WINTER

SEASONS OF THE YEAR

Harriet Brundle

KU-130-522

SEASONS OF THE YEAR

©2016
Book Life
King's Lynn
Norfolk
PE30 4LS

ISBN: 978-1-910512-57-9

All rights reserved
Printed in China

Written by:
Harriet Brundle

Edited by:
Gemma McMullen

Designed by:
Drue Rintoul

A catalogue record for this book
is available from the British Library.

WITHDRAWN FROM

Bromley Libraries

30128 80235 155 4

Contents

Words that appear like this can be found in the glossary on page 24.

Seasons of the Year

There are four seasons in a year. The seasons are called Spring, Summer, Autumn and Winter.

Each season is different. This book will tell you about Winter!

5

Winter

Winter happens after Autumn. The Winter months are December, January and February.

Winter

January

Sun	Mon	Tue	Wed	Thu	Fri	Sat
1	2	3	4	5	6	7
8	9	10	11	12	13	14
15	16	17	18	19	20	21
22	23	24	25	26	27	28
29	30	31				

February

Sun	Mon	Tue	Wed	Thu	Fri	Sat
			1	2	3	4
5	6	7	8	9	10	11
12	13	14	15	16	17	18
19	20	21	22	23	24	25
26	27	28	29			

March

Sun	Mon	Tue	Wed	Thu	Fri	Sat
			1	2	3	
4	5	6	7	8	9	10
11	12	13	14	15	16	17
18	19	20	21	22	23	24
25	26	27	28	29	30	31

April

Sun	Mon	Tue	Wed	Thu	Fri	Sat
	2	3	4	5	6	7
	9	10	11	12	13	14
	16	17	18	19	20	21
	23	24	25	26	27	28
	30					

May

Sun	Mon	Tue	Wed	Thu	Fri	Sat
		1	2	3	4	5
6	7	8	9	10	11	12
13	14	15	16	17	18	19
20	21	22	23	24	25	26
27	28	29	30	31		

June

Sun	Mon	Tue	Wed	Thu	Fri	Sat
					1	2
3	4	5	6	7	8	9
10	11	12	13	14	15	16
17	18	19	20	21	22	23
24	25	26	27	28	29	30

July

Sun	Mon	Tue	Wed	Thu	Fri	Sat
	2	3	4	5	6	7
	9	10	11	12	13	14
	16	17	18	19	20	21
	23	24	25	26	27	28
	30	31				

August

Sun	Mon	Tue	Wed	Thu	Fri	Sat
			1	2	3	4
	6	7	8	9	10	11
	13	14	15	16	17	18
	20	21	22	23	24	25
	27	28	29	30	31	

September

Sun	Mon	Tue	Wed	Thu	Fri	Sat
						1
2	3	4	5	6	7	8
9	10	11	12	13	14	15
16	17	18	19	20	21	22
23	24	25	26	27	28	29
30						

October

Sun	Mon	Tue	Wed	Thu	Fri	Sat

November

Sun	Mon	Tue	Wed	Thu	Fri	Sat

December

Sun	Mon	Tue	Wed	Thu	Fri	Sat

There are less hours of sunshine in Winter than in any other season. This makes the daytime feel shorter.

The Weather

The weather is very cold in Winter. It is wet and windy.

Frost

Sometimes there is snow in Winter.
It feels very cold to touch.

Be careful not to slip on ice!

9

Plants

Some plants die in Winter.
The weather is too cold for
them to stay alive.

10

Branches

Trunk

Most trees lose their leaves.
We can see their trunks and branches.

Animals

Some animals migrate in Winter.
Birds fly to places that are warmer.

Other animals hibernate in Winter. They find a safe place and sleep through the cold weather.

In the Garden

It is fun to plant seeds and bulbs in Winter. The plants will grow as the weather gets warmer.

When there is snow, we can make a snowman in the garden!

Food

Lots of vegetables are ready to be eaten in Winter.

Which other vegetables do you like to eat in the Winter?

Broccoli

Carrots

Onions

We can use Winter vegetables to make meals such as soup and stew.

17

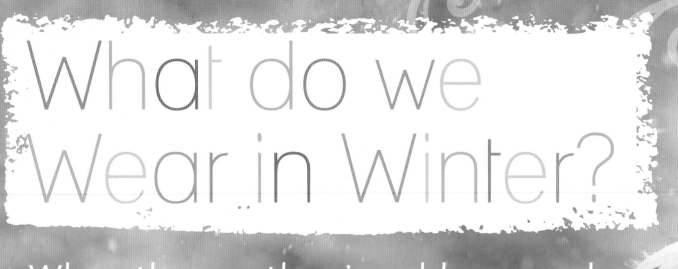

What do we Wear in Winter?

When the weather is cold we need to stay warm. We wear gloves to keep our hands warm.

Rain Coat

When it rains we wear our rain coats so we don't get wet.

Things to do in Winter

In December, many people celebrate Christmas. It is fun to decorate a Christmas tree.

We can go to the woods and collect pine cones and chestnuts!

21

Facts about Winter

Did you know?

Each snowflake looks different to the next one.

In some places there is cold weather
all year round! The North Pole and South Pole
are places on Earth where there is always snow.

23

Glossary

Bulbs: the part that plants grow from.

Decorate: to add something to an object to make it look better.

Hibernate: to spend the Winter sleeping.

Migrate: move from one place to another.

Photo credits

Photocredits: Abbreviations: l-left, r-right, b-bottom, t-top, c-centre, m-middle. All images are courtesy of Shutterstock.com.
Front Cover – FamVeld. 1, 24 – ISchmidt. 2 - Daniel J. Rao. 3 - Jeka. 4l Konstanttin. 4lc – djgis. 4rc – Smileus. 4r – Triff. 5 - MNStudio. 7 - Halfbottle. 7 - LilKar. 8 - Algefoto. 8inset - Amy Johansson. 9 - Nadezda Cruzova. 9inset - Robsonphoto. 10 - Glenn Young. 10inset - AlinaMD. 11 - fotografos. 12 - rootstock. 13 - Nemeziya. 14 - gorillaimages. 14inset - Kim Doucette. 15 - oliveromg. 16l - chanwangrong. 16c - Christian Delbert. 16r - D7INAMI7S. 17 - Ildi Papp. 17inset - Mindy w.m. Chung. 18 - Alena Ozerova. 19 - MNStudio. 20 - Pressmaster. 21 - Sergey Peterman. 21bl - Wollertz. 21br - SamKent12. 22 - Elovich. 23 - Volodymyr Goinyk.